Friends FOREVER?

why your friendships are so important

Friends FOREVER?

why your friendships are so important

by Odile Amblard
illustrated by Andrée Prigent
edited by Andrea Bussell

sunscreen

Library of Congress Cataloging-in-Publication Data:
Amblard, Odile.
Friends forever? : why your friendships are so important /
by Odile Amblard ; illustrated by Andrée Prigent ; edited by Andrea Bussell.
p. cm. — (Sunscreen)
ISBN-13: 978-0-8109-9480-5 (harry n. abrams)
1. Friendship in adolescence. 2. Interpersonal relations in adolescence.
I. Prigent, Andrée. II. Bussell, Andrea. III. Title.
BF724.3.F64A43 2008
158.2'5—dc22
2007043138

Text copyright © 2008 Odile Amblard
Illustrations © 2008 Andrée Prigent

Translated by Nicholas Elliott

Book series design by Higashi Glaser Design

Published in 2008 by Amulet Books, an imprint of Harry N. Abrams, Inc.

Printed and bound in China
10 9 8 7 6 5 4 3 2 1

HNA ▮▯▯▯▯
harry n. abrams, inc.
a subsidiary of La Martinière Groupe
115 West 18th Street
New York, NY 10011
www.hnabooks.com

contents

WHAT IS
FRIENDSHIP?
WHY DO
WE MAKE
FRIENDS?
WHAT MAKES
THEM SO
IMPORTANT?

It's hard to describe why you have the friends you do, right? Even though you experience friendships every day of your life, you don't talk about them, you live them. It's as simple as that.

Sociologists and psychologists all agree that our reasons for connecting with one another are mysterious, and no amount of scientific data could do a better job of explaining friendship. The famous French writer Montaigne described why he chose one of his friends like this: "Because he is who he is, because I am who I am."

Don't worry, this short book isn't going to analyze or dissect friendship—that would be too boring. The purpose of this book is to hold a mirror to your own great friendships so you can understand them better and to help you open doors to new ones. Because forming friendships is one of the most exciting journeys of life.

everybody's
a buddy

lots of
acquaintances,
a handful of
true friends

a fortunate meeting

the tale of the lobster

FRIENDSHIP
IS ESSENTIAL

the rhythms
of friendship

everybody's a
buddy

From the time you're twelve to the time you're eighteen, you're constantly surrounded by different types of friends: really close friends (the ones you can count on a single hand), friends from your classes at school, friends from your neighborhood, and friends from the activities you do after school. Of course, you are probably closer to some friends than to others, but you all have things in common that draw you together. For instance, you all spend the day together in the same school or hang out in the same place, and you all have a home where your family is waiting for you. But most of you probably spend much less time with your parents than you do with your friends. You're transitioning from childhood to young adulthood, and from your home life to your life at school and beyond. Everything is changing. Who else could understand what you're going through better than someone who is going through exactly the same thing? Times like these are what make friends so important.

In school, for example, you and your classmates are all "friends" when it comes to standing up for yourselves against adults—teachers, supervisors, coaches, etc. Even if you don't get along with everybody in your class, you'd rather stick together than tattle on each other because you're all having a similar experience. Despite your differences, you understand each other in this crazy universe of grades and homework, lunchroom shenanigans, passing notes in history class, and running laps in the gym. You and your classmates know that it's your time together that makes school bearable sometimes. It feels good to be with your friends.

lots of acquaintances, a handful of
true friends

So, you have fun with your friends, acquaintances, classmates, and neighbors. You have the same schedules and teachers, and sometimes the same problems; sometimes you even travel together as a team to play in basketball tournaments. That's all great, but what does it mean? It might be fun to pull pranks or play the rival school's team together, but are these kinds of friendships enough to make you truly happy? Can you confide in those friends or call them after a bad day? Probably not, which is why having close friends means so much.

A close friend is someone who adds meaning to your life. He's the one who knows all your favorite bands and rents your favorite movies with you, even if he doesn't like all of them himself. She's the one who helps you deal with getting yelled at by your dad because you put on a little too much eyeliner this morning, or because you played your stereo too loudly while he was watching a ball game.

Between the two of you, there's much more than just a casual "Hey, how's it going" by your lockers or a "If you lend me your math homework, I'll help you with the science assignment." Even playing video games together seems to mean something more. The conversation flows. You have nothing to hide. You love listening to what he or she has to say.

Imagine your relationships as the circles created by a rock skipping across a pond. The farthest circle would be your neighborhood gang, your classmates would be in the next closest circle, and the kids on your sports team would be in the closest one after that. Your good friends would be even closer. Then, closest of all, you'd find your best friend or friends. You might jump from one circle to another, depending

on your schedule or how you feel. But your best friends are a different story. The important thing isn't that they belong to a certain circle; the important thing is that they are with you. It doesn't matter whether you have class or practice together, because your connection exists by itself and you don't need a reason to hang out!

a fortunate meeting

Some friendships begin in funny ways: because of a vicious fight between two twelve-year-olds in the penalty zone of the soccer field, or from a teacher separating two "chatterboxes" and assigning them to new lab partners, or just from two kids being randomly assigned lockers next to each other. Sociologists and psychologists have never been able to establish the causes of friendship, so they humbly fall back on a simple definition: Friendship begins with an encounter between two people. But why a certain pair at a specific moment? Nobody knows. We can all dream up possible explanations for our friendships, but we may never find the true reasons. Sure, he likes computers and swimming, just like you do. Okay, she goes to the same high school and lives on the same block as you. So what? Don't you know plenty of other people who meet those criteria? What about that girl whose dad works with your dad? You always played together when you were kids, but you're not *friends*, right?

good-bye, childhood

You probably hear it from a lot of adults, most likely doctors and therapists: "Friendship is essential, especially when you're a teenager!" And you can't stand it when they get going with their pseudoscientific babble. After all, you're the one who knows all about being a teenager.

But in truth, what they have to say about friends and the role friendship plays in your development is really pretty relevant. Your friends are becoming increasingly important because sometimes—or all the time, depending on the day—you feel like your parents just don't get it. It's like they're standing on the other side of a fence; they're nothing like you.

ph1

Once upon a time, when you were little, you used to see them differently. Your parents were amazing and strong and beautiful. They were perfect! Of course, you probably didn't say that to yourself, but any psychology book will tell you that when you're a child you use your parents as role models—ideal models for who you will become. Then, little by little, that model has to be broken down so you can learn how to be you, even though it sometimes hurts. Change is hard, but that's what being a teenager is all about. As a teenager, you start to understand that one day you'll have to leave your parents and make your own way. Whether you're conscious of it or not, you start seeing your parents in a different light, and you have to. In order to grow up, to become who you are, you need to get some perspective. They're them and you're you. To find your own place, you need to find a way to put your parents in the background. But it's certainly not as easy as it sounds.

the tale of the
lobster

In her book *Words for Adolescents*, the famous French psychoanalyst Françoise Dolto found an apt metaphor for this stage of life:

> *When lobsters change shells, they start by losing the old ones and remain defenseless while they grow new ones. During this period, they are in great danger. Teenagers have a very similar experience. It takes a lot of sweat and tears to grow a new shell. . . . Adolescence is like the lobster changing its shell.*

During such a weird time, it's only natural that teenagers should turn to other people who are having the same experiences they are: their friends. When you're a teenager, your friends play a more important role in your life because they can relate to what you're going through.

When you're feeling fragile—when you're without your "shell"—you need people around you to help you protect yourself. You need your friends. With them, you can form a united front, and they can make you feel confident and strong. You can recognize your own struggles and fears in their lives, sort of like a reflection in a mirror. And you can learn from them by seeing how they face the same things you do.

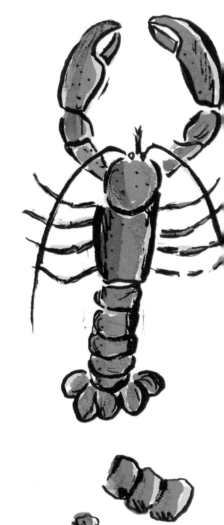

The mirror provided by relationships is important, because even if you're not fully aware of the transformation you're going through as a teenager, it's still pretty profound. One day, you look in an actual mirror and don't recognize yourself—your nose seems bigger, your mouth is too wide, your chest is developing, your mustache keeps getting darker, you've got new pimples. It's scary and it can be upsetting. One day you feel great—life is beautiful and the future is bright. Then the next day— *wham!*—everything collapses. This morning you were laughing at a comic book; tonight you'll be choking back tears while you watch *Titanic* on TV. Sometimes adolescence is an emotional roller coaster!

Are you the only one who suffers like this? No way! Talking to your friends—sometimes even just looking at them—can provide sweet relief because they can reassure you that they're going through the same changes you are.

say no to
loneliness

Adolescence is a time to make friends and hang out in groups, but it can also be a time of complex loneliness. Though friendships tend to become deeper during your teenage years, a feeling of loneliness can also become more intense. Think about it: Now that your friends are at the core of your emotional life, you become more sensitive to being separated from them. You also begin exploring your own feelings. You question the world around you and begin searching for the meaning of life. As a teenager, you say good-bye to childhood, when everyone is a friend, and you become more careful about choosing the people you want to have as your friends. You also suffer if you don't have any.

There are different degrees of loneliness. Feeling lonely or sad because you're stuck in your room, far from your group of friends, isn't the end of the world—you know you'll see them again soon. But what if your best friend moves away? Or if you feel like you just can't make friends? In these kinds of situations, loneliness is much harder to handle. The worst thing you could do would be to just accept it, to tell yourself, "This is just how it is—I don't want another friend because no one can replace her" or "I can't have any friends because I don't know how to make them."

It's not true! If you give up trying to form friendships when you're twelve, fifteen, or seventeen, what will you do when you're thirty, forty, or fifty? Will you just stay cooped up by yourself at home? No! Adolescence is the ideal time in your life to learn how to make friends, because everyone else is learning how to as well. It's easier to learn how to come out of your shell when you're fifteen than it is when you're forty-five, so do it now!

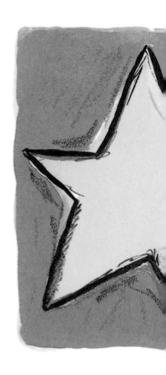

self-confidence

Is it that difficult to make friends? It is if you aren't confident. When you're not really sure who you are because of all of the changes taking place in your body and mind, you can easily get freaked out by the idea of "being yourself" around other people. You might think you have nothing to offer to others, but being a good friend is the best and most important thing you can give.

ph1

Some say, "The only way to have a friend is to be one." Are you a good friend? Would you say you're interested in others? Are you a good listener? Are you trustworthy and open? Do you focus on the positive things about yourself and others? Even if you need to work on a few things (like keeping secrets when you've promised

to, or not interrupting someone when they're talking), chances are you're still a pretty good friend. That's something to be confident about!

Everyone has shortcomings; some people just hide them better than others. Don't be afraid to display your strong points. Let other people enjoy them. If you do, making friends might be a little easier than you thought.

being open to
friendship

There's no miracle cure for a lack of confidence, but to come out of your shell, you have to make the first move. For example, your middle school or junior high must have a sports team, or clubs devoted to the yearbook, debating, computers, or some other activity that you enjoy. Signing up for one of these activities can be a good way to meet people. The same goes for your hometown—wouldn't the basketball courts, the local theater, or the local library be great places to make friends and meet people?

A lack of self-confidence can be overwhelming. It can even make you feel afraid of other people. In these cases, there's no quick-and-easy solution. The best thing to do is gather your courage and talk to an adult you trust. Or,

seek out an adult who really knows how to listen, like a psychologist or a guidance counselor. Every city has resources you can draw on—ask your school nurse or your doctor, or get some information from the Internet. And you can always try talking to your parents. A single conversation won't solve everything, but it can give you the advice and encouragement you need to move forward.

the rhythms of
friendship

€ven if you make the first move to come out of your shell and meet new people, you won't always find a true friend right away. Sometimes what you thought was a solid friendship might only last a few weeks or months. Why? Probably because adolescence is a period of rapid transformations both in mind and in body. As psychologists like to say, "People mature at

different speeds." That doesn't mean that a friendship that has come to an end wasn't worth anything. Friendship, like love, can take time and practice. It's natural for people to have a variety of romantic relationships before they find the "love of their life." Time and experience give you a better grasp on love and on who you are. Friendship is a lot like that. You may need to have several friendships before you realize what you're looking for in a good friend. You can learn from all of them.

phase

2

bosom buddies: little things and big laughs

similarities:
two peas in a pod

differences:
two halves of a whole

confidants:
you tell each
other everything

tolerance: you don't judge each other

DAY-TO-DAY FRIENDSHIP

loyalty: you never turn your back

bosom buddies:
little things
and
big laughs

Friendship can change any situation and make it better. Even your chores can be kind of fun if you do them with a friend! (Well, almost.)

Your boring classes can be events to look forward to if your friends are also in them—you can always pass notes or roll your eyes at one another! And what about the times when you and your friend have told each other everything there is to tell and should be bored, but still manage to find things to talk about for countless hours?

Take, for example, athletes who play on sports teams. Their friendships are strengthened by attending practice sessions together after school and

ph2

by playing regional tournaments and championships all over the state on weekends. The weariness that comes from repeating the same movement a thousand times, the tension before the game, the extreme concentration required for championship matches, the intensity of the face-off, the delirium of victory, the despair of defeat—those are some powerful shared experiences! No matter what it is you're doing when you're with your friends, it takes on a new significance and becomes an even more powerful memory when you revisit it together: "Remember that time in Boise when you slam-dunked ten seconds before the bell?"

When you and a friend are together, you're both a little braver, egging each other on and testing your limits. Maybe you push each other in a relay race at the track meet. Maybe you learn new things from each other by exchanging books and CDs. Or maybe you lock yourselves in your bedroom and organize a private karaoke party where you sing, dance, and end up rolling on the floor, squealing with laughter.

Friendship can be rich with a thousand memories of hilarious and mischievous times. A teacher or a friend might say something

seemingly innocent and you lose control. Your laughter mixes with your friend's and builds to a frenzy. The sound of your friend laughing makes you laugh even harder, and vice versa. You wish it would never stop.

similarities:

two peas in a pod

"*Those who resemble each other, assemble,*" according to the saying. Is that really true? Do great friendships happen because you meet someone who's a lot like you? You certainly need some mutual interests: a passion for video games or ballet, a shared love of Kurt Cobain, or a similar loathing of Top 40 music. You might have similar tastes in clothes or books, or you might just happen to crack the same jokes in similar situations. On the other hand, you may have other similarities that aren't very pleasant. You can develop a closer, more intimate relationship with a friend because you're both going through similar  situations at home—your parents might be separating or your dads might be out of work. Though they're hard to live through alone, those kinds of situations give you a sense of belonging when you're with each other. You don't have to explain yourselves, because you each know the other person is probably feeling the same way and might not want to talk about it. You both know it sometimes helps to remain quiet and just be there to support each other until one of you wants to let it all out.

But deep friendship can also be rooted in your differences as much as it is in your similarities. If you're a total hothead, you might admire your friend's patience. You might envy her work ethic when you feel lazy. You might appreciate her quietness, while she loves your outrageous sense of humor. Eventually, without noticing, you pass from a phase of wanting to be more like your friend to a stage where you deliberately cultivate and appreciate your small differences. Doesn't a sports team's strength lie in the way the players complement each other, rather than in their individual performances? The same thing goes for friendship—your differences can be more valuable than your similarities!

differences:

two halves of a whole

Even though you appreci-ate your own uniqueness, some-times you need to feel like you resemble your friends, because it's through them that you'll understand yourself a little better and like yourself a little more. But growing up is not about losing yourself in similarities or fading into a crowd. Growing up is about becoming yourself. Friendships should help you do this by teaching you to recognize your strengths and weaknesses. Your friendships should teach you and your friends to appreciate each other the way you are.

One of the best things in life is getting to know someone and allowing yourself to be surprised by what you learn from them. Another person can lead you on journeys you would have never taken alone. Without your friend, you might never have given the writers Kerouac, Ginsberg, or Burroughs a second glance. She might be someone who will read anything she can get her hands on, from Flaubert's *Madame Bovary* to Toni Morrison's *Beloved*, but you might prefer to watch a movie twice a week. Differences like these can teach you to compare points of view and maybe allow you to change your mind about something you thought you were sure of.

What's great about friendship is that your differences can separate you and bring you closer together at the same time. You and your friend can find what you're lacking in each other. You might have angelic patience when it comes to explaining a math assignment, and she might be able to keep up a good mood when yours starts to waver. Encountering these differences helps you to learn about tolerance, respect, and reasoning together.

confidants:

you tell each other everything

Friendship is trust. You know that you can tell your best friend everything. That's why she's your friend and not just an acquaintance. With acquaintances, you chat, have some laughs, and sometimes even get into arguments. But with a best friend, words go further. You can tell your best friend about a crush without worrying that the whole lunchroom will know about it in half an hour. You can also trust your best friend with all the intimate details about yourself that you'd never tell anyone else: the way you feel about your acne, how much you don't like your skinny legs, or the fact that you often get up to eat in the middle of the night. You tell a real friend everything you couldn't possibly tell anyone else. A true friend has a different way of listening. She's discreet, attentive, and, most important, she keeps

her mouth shut when it comes to your secrets! Without saying a word, at some point a pact was made: what passes between us is confidential. Thanks to this promise, you can pour your heart out. You're not ashamed to reveal your anxieties, such as your fear of growing up in such a complicated world, or your fear of your parents divorcing. And you're not afraid of revealing what you're ashamed of: you think your body's weird, you think you don't have anything interesting to say in your literature class, you're depressed. With your friend, you don't get hung up about showing all the different parts of yourself. Sometimes you tease each other about the things that bother you most because you understand each other, and together you can laugh about your problems without ever being hurtful.

no need for
words

You might spend hours on end talking with your friend about your boyfriends or girlfriends and swapping secrets. You can talk about your doubts: "Does he really like me? Do I really like her? How come sometimes I don't feel comfortable around him?" And if you're not talking about your crushes, you're talking about yourself.

From the silliest things to the most important, from the funniest things to the most disgusting, you can talk about anything with your friend because her or she is someone you know how to talk to; someone you *can* talk to, with no holds barred. The more you talk, the more you have to say to each other—that's the magic of friendship! But even when you're quiet, you're still communicating! You think about what you just told each other, what you're going to tell each other, even what you won't tell each other. And you can be fine with just sitting in silence because you're so comfortable being together.

tolerance:
you don't judge each other

Have you ever done something stupid and immediately wished you hadn't? Like taking ten dollars from your grandmother's purse, or accusing your little sister of breaking your mom's perfume bottle when you were the one who did it, or snapping at your teacher during a bad day? In other words, think about something you've done that's relatively serious and that you're not proud of. Those are situations in which your friend can be completely amazing. You know that if he doesn't agree with you or if he criticizes you, he's only doing those things because he respects you, not because he thinks he's better than you are. So with him you don't have to pretend. You let it all out without worrying that he'll make fun of you or judge you, and he reacts as naturally as can be, exactly how you thought he would. He might change the subject to your upcoming trip to the ice-skating rink next Saturday or tell you about the time he did something much worse, something he's never told anyone about before. Not only does a friend avoid cutting you down, he understands you. Completely.

Friends don't judge each other. They know how useless that is. There are already enough people giving you sermons: teachers, parents, neighbors, even well-intentioned friends. When you don't agree with your friend, he or she doesn't take it badly; you accept each other as you are. But that doesn't mean you let each other get away with just about anything because you don't want to be judgmental. That would not be friendship, either. Friends never avoid debating or disagreeing! Isn't telling someone, "I wouldn't do that" or "I'm worried you're making a mistake and might hurt yourself" a sign of love and respect? Of course, there's a right way and a wrong way to say that kind of thing, but it's essential that friends don't fake it. Sometimes everyone needs a little guidance and good advice, and that's what friends are for!

loyalty:
you never turn your back

The sadness of separation and the joy of being reunited—they are the yin and yang of friendship. When you go to the same school and you have the same class schedule, you wind up spending a lot of time together, to the point where you have a hard time parting ways to go home and have dinner and do your homework, or to go on vacation with your family. You'd almost rather skip those vacations and stay in school just to be able to see each other! Almost. (Let's not overdo it.) When you think about it, it's not so hard to bridge distances. All you need is a telephone or a stamped envelope or Internet access.

The cell phone is definitely friendship's number one ally. Even though it brings you closer to your friends, it doesn't necessarily bring you closer to your parents, right? Don't say you've never seen your dad gasp when he opens the phone bill! Every month the threats are unleashed: "If you keep this up, we're taking away your phone!" Or the more insidious: "We're going to make you pay your own bills!" But let's be honest—you never really feel like you're doing anything wrong in the first place! You get home from school, and even though you said good-bye to your friend barely twenty minutes ago, you suddenly have to speak to her. On the walk home, you ran into what's-his-face with what's-her-name and that's a news flash you just can't sit on. Or you're on the couch watching your favorite TV show and you can't resist talking about it together. Or you might really and truly need help with your math homework . . . so there's really no choice but to call her for help. Of course, not all your calls are devoted to gossip and school. When everything feels like it's collapsing and you feel like a nobody, the phone turns into a life jacket and your conversation becomes a rescue operation.

Sometimes talking on the phone is even better than if you were together sitting side by side—it's like the distance allows you to be more open. Maybe you don't try to hold back the tears. Maybe your friend finds just the right words to comfort you or knows you'd rather he just listen. But the phone isn't the only way to be more open with each other.

notes and
e-mails

If you like to write, you're in luck! You've got an easy option: e-mails! Of course, if you see your friend in school all the time you're not going to send her an essay every day, or even every week.

If you're writing to a friend, you don't question whether you like writing or if you're any good at it. You just do it. You write long e-mails that combine the trivial with the essential. When you're on vacation and are far apart, letters and e-mails express what you usually wouldn't say to each other—everyday details, such as who you're hanging out with and every last story. Distance often erases shyness. You might sign a letter, "Your friend for life," but would you say that out loud? Have you ever cut interesting advertisements out of a magazine to turn them into personalized notes or envelopes? Depending on your mood, you'll decorate a plain page with clouds of smoke or country landscapes, or you'll simply create your own stationery, designing the shape, mixing materials and colors. You don't have to rely solely on words to express yourself!

life is better when you're
together

Calling and writing each other are great, but they're no replacement for actually seeing each other. As with talking on the phone, any excuse is a good one when it comes to spending more time together. The most obvious choice is working together: doing your math homework or preparing an oral presentation on *To Kill a Mockingbird*. Your collaborations can be enriching for both your minds and your friendship.

But there's more to life than studying! There are parties, weekends, and vacations. These are ideal opportunities for spending time together (as long as your parents are OK with it). Sometimes you might stay over at her place, and other times she might camp out in your room. You might negotiate with your parents so your friend can come with you to visit your grandparents or go on vacations with you. But when you live with someone twenty-four-seven, you quickly find out if you *really* get along with them. So if you want to have a good vacation, be sure you're confident in your friend and your friendship. When you are, that's the greatest. His house is your house, his family adopts you, your family adopts him. And you barely ever have to leave each other.

solidarity:

you stick together

Who do you call at 10 P.M. with a broken heart? Who will give you the perfect alibi to get your mom off your back so you can sneak off to the movies with your date for the first time? Whose place do you go to so you can read *Us Weekly*, *In Touch*, and *Star*, those celebrity trash "rags" your mom doesn't want to see in the house? Who will always be there to take you by the arm and get you a soda after you get yelled at for talking in math class? A true friend is always there. Popular wisdom has it that "You recognize your friends in times of trial." Your friend is the person you can ask anything of, anytime, anyplace.

never letting go

𝒩o matter what, friends don't drop each other. They know what to do to make each other feel better. Two years ago, when your parents got divorced and your whole world fell apart, how would you have made it without her? At first, you didn't talk about it. But without asking a single question, your friend helped you recover. Sometimes she offered to let you do your homework at her house so you didn't have to go right back to a home you hated. On weekends, she offered to take you to the pool, or even grocery shopping, just so you could be away from what was hurting you. Later, you found out she was the one who told your teachers what was going on so that they wouldn't be too tough on you during the worst of it. Whether it's a real crisis or a small case of the blues, true friends stick together. A friend is someone who will invite you

over to watch the latest Spielberg movie when you don't make the football team. He doesn't make a big deal out of it. He knows you're having a hard time, so he'll do whatever he can to distract you until you feel better.

Words cannot describe the solidarity between the two of you, and you don't need to weather a crisis to prove the bond is there. It strengthens with every passing day through little gestures and signs. One day, you listen to him bare his soul and you reassure him. The next week, it's you who calls him for support when you're devastated after another fight with your girlfriend. He's the only one who knows what to say. When you tried to tell your big brother about it, he nearly laughed in your face: "Get rid of that chick. There's plenty of fish in the sea!" No one else seems to understand.

You're so good at cheering each other up because you're on the same wavelength. You don't have to search for words—you find them right away. You're never afraid of bothering each other. That's what you're there for—each other.

quotes

"Friendship is the center of my life."
—BRIAN

"Without her, the schoolyard was enormous and scary."
—GAIL

"A real friend is like oxygen."
—JULIE

"When you have a case of the blues, a friend makes everything all right."
—MARION

"Acquaintances run in packs, a true friend stands apart."
—JAN

"If we didn't have friends, we'd keep everything to ourselves."
—CARRIE

"Your friend is there for you anytime, anyplace."
—MURIEL

"At parties, even though there are tons of people, you're always looking for your friend."
—BRIDGET

"Your friend accepts you the way you are and you're not afraid of letting him down."
—ARNOLD

"Your friend knows you like the back of his own hand."
—ERICA

"You can go away on vacation with a friend for a month and still get along."
—FRANKIE

"There are 'hello and good-bye' friendships, and REAL friendships."
—DEBBIE

girlfriends: BFFs!

guy friends: all for one and one for all

girls and guys: can they really be "just friends"?

cliques and groups
safety in numbers
or just another fish
in the sea?

three's company:
you, your friend,
and her boyfriend

YOU AND

OTHERS

parents:
friends or
foes?

guy friends:

all for one and one for all

Friendship between boys and girls consists of trust, under-standing, and openness. But they usually express it differently. Friendship between girls tends to be more intimate and emotional. Between boys, friendship just "is." They don't really talk about it.

Why are friendships between boys and girls different? Because boys and girls are raised differently! For example, wasn't your father taught that a man doesn't cry? Aren't women and girls supposed to be chatterboxes? And don't boys call their friends "little girls" if they complain they got hurt in a school-yard

tussle? Even though lots of things have changed over time—schools are now coed and women are now able to do just as much as men—a lot of people still think this way.

Girls and boys have different ways of expressing their feelings. For instance, teenage girls love to analyze their friendships and describe their moods, while boys usually don't say much about that sort of thing. Friendships between boys don't often rely on talk. They are often less intimate and exclusive. Groups of four, five, or six good friends are fairly common among boys.

Girls tend to go in pairs, sometimes in trios. Guys tend to be drawn together by activities. There's school, of course, but also sports and hobbies: video games, computers, and movies. These are things that don't require a lot of talk! Is that why squabbles, jealousy, and gossip aren't as much of a problem between boys?

girlfriends:
bffs!

"Over time, a sense of identity, the idea that we were alike in every way, settled in. We were constantly stunned to discover that we had underlined the same word or passage in a book. That we were both touched by the same aspect of a person's face. We lost count of the number of times we expressed the same wish at the same moment, noticed that we had the same flaw, the same habit." (Fabrice Lardeau, *Paper Sheets*, Denoël, 1994)

You've probably already guessed that these are the words of a young girl. Who she is doesn't matter. She could be you or one of your friends. She speaks for all those who have strongly experienced friendship. Her words are a good example of the ways girls describe and analyze their relationships. They place emphasis on stability, duration, and depth. Girls care for each other openly, straightforwardly. They don't need to hide their feelings.

Female friendship is synonymous with intimacy—there is a closeness that increases from one secret to the next. We've all come across a pair of girlfriends who are inseparable. They arrive at school together or meet by the entrance and never leave each other. They sit side by side in class, think together, and speak in a single voice. They laugh when kids gently tease them by calling them the "Siamese twins" because they're so happy to have discovered what it means to "find your soul mate."

three's company:
you, your friend, and her boyfriend

You share everything with a friend: your time, your fun, your troubles, and your dreams. But is it possible to share yourself? For example, is it possible to give equal parts of yourself to a friend *and* to a boyfriend? Or are you ready to share your friend with her boyfriend? In theory, yes, of course! But in day-to-day reality, things can get a little more complicated.

Often, at the beginning of a close friendship, you don't want to spend time with anyone but your new friend. You don't think you need anyone else, and you hope nothing will ever come between the two of you.

But what happens when suddenly your best friend has a boyfriend? You might feel left behind. And what if the boyfriend complains that he feels like he's taking second place to his girlfriend's best friend? Suddenly you're overwhelmed with sadness or even anger. You feel betrayed, maybe even humiliated. You start to forget that friendship is a matter of mutual choice, and that the other person didn't *steal* your friend. Your friend has developed a new relationship with someone else.

Sometimes this can lead to crying fits, fights, or sulking contests. We may need time to learn that we should never try to own our friends. Sometimes our foolish pride can lead us to believe that we can be all a friend needs. But think about it: how can you want your friend to be happy (which you know you do) *and* consider depriving her of the joy of being in love? That makes no sense at all.

girls and guys:
can they really be "just friends"?

Do you believe in friendship between boys and girls? Even if you haven't experienced it, you've certainly seen it happen. That kind of friendship—like all relationships—is special. It's special because it's different. It has all the qualities of your other friendships—understanding, trust, loyalty. It allows you to be open and to learn about yourself from a new perspective—a boy's perspective if you're a girl, or a girl's perspective if you're a boy—and that's necessary!

But this kind of friendship can also be fragile when you're trying to discover who you really are, since part of your identity involves flirting. Sometimes a friendship with someone of the opposite sex can make you feel insecure or cause you to question yourself, especially if you find that you are attracted to the other person. Dating a friend can be a great experience because of the friendship you've already built, but it can also change things pretty drastically.

Friendships with people of the opposite sex are like emotional adventures, and they can be fascinating and enriching. Of course you'd like to avoid certain mistakes that leave your heart aching, but whose advice would you really listen to? You can take advantage of a friend's experience or listen to a parent's opinion, but sometimes you have to find out for yourself. And honestly, it's better that way! Wouldn't it be kind of sad never to experience something for yourself because someone you know might have had a difficult experience?

cliques
and groups:
safety in numbers, or just another fish in the sea?

Those who belong to a large group of genuine friends will tell you how great it is to be able to have many different people to hang out with. They all feel good together, are ready to stand by each other in case of trouble, and are never really alone. But group friendships can also be a little suffocating from time to time. Groups can help to create new pairs of friends who will then leave the group to get to know each other better, but they can also stifle special relationships or even individuality.

THE PROS: Being in a group can create a spirit of solidarity and power that strengthens every one of its members and reinforces self-confidence; it can teach you to be tolerant and ensure that you have tons of fun!

THE CONS: Being in a group can completely wipe out your individuality. You might know you're really different from the others, but might not feel strong enough to express that difference, becase you want everyone to like you. When you're not sure who you are, you might live through the others and act like they do so you won't be alone.

But what if the group dissolves? And what if, by imitating the others, you wind up erasing important parts of yourself? Luckily, by the time you ask yourself these questions, they've usually resolved themselves. It's difficult to think about these things when you can't get much distance from the group. But those things are all part of your path in life, and before you know it, you've all found your own way—one of you is in college, one is studying abroad, one has a job, and another one has joined the army!

parents:
friends or foes?

We all have parents, and they're all different: there are over-protective parents, workaholic parents, parents who don't see that their kids are growing up, terrible parents, terrifying parents, and single parents. Whatever they're like, your parents will try to get to know all the friends who become a part of your life. Your mom and dad might have prepared themselves for playing a small part in your teenage years, but it still makes them feel strange to see you grow up. Sometimes you hug them like you used to, sometimes you ignore them. This is normal. It's your friends who'll help get you through your teenage years, not just your parents. Your friends are going through the same changes you are. It isn't surprising to learn that two sociologists estimated that you'll spend twice as much time in your life with your friends as you will with your parents. But you don't spend the same *kind* of time with your parents as you do with your friends. With friends, you ponder the same questions and you face the same fears. You're 100 percent

in the moment. With your parents, you weave a family experience made up of thousands of threads. Your parents consider life in the past, present, and future tenses—especially the future. They can't help it. It's their job to guide you toward your future. Hence their interest in your grades, and the growing tension when college preparations appear on the horizon or when you have to decide what job will be best for you.

in private

A poll taken by a magazine revealed that the biggest problem between you and your parents is your schooling. When your classes are going well—your teachers like you, and you're getting good grades—peace reigns. But if your grades are looking sketchy, beware. You probably know your parents' anger can extend to your friends. If something isn't going well at school, you're partially to blame in your parents' minds, but so are your friends. They take up all your time, don't they? And they influence you.

In general, parents and friends recognize their respective territories. Your parents deal with your studies, plans for the future, and relationships. Your friends influence your musical tastes, hobbies, and way of speaking. But you may have a hard time keeping those boundaries straight and your parents happy.

Your parents might come to see your friends as rivals. Sometimes their desire to "help" does more harm than good: they might read your mail, snoop around your room, call your friend after you've had a fight with her, or play buddy-buddy with whomever you bring home. But your parents may need some time to get used to the older, more mature you. You constantly surprise them. They thought you were different or think you're still a kid. Raising your voice to assert yourself, slamming a door, or leaving a note on the rug in their bedroom can make the point. If your relationship takes a turn for the worse, you might know an adult who could discreetly intervene: an aunt, a friend of your parents in whom you have complete confidence, or a doctor. Your parents need to learn to cut the umbilical cord, and you might have to help them figure out how!

4

phase

brothers
and sisters
beloved
enemies

your parents:
your friends?

dear diary

mentors

REAL FRIENDS/
FAKE FRIENDS

moving
away?

your friend flicka

Everyone has his or her special blanket, blue-eyed doll, or worn-out teddy bear with cuddly fur, who's always there for them like the most practical and attentive of friends; a friend who sticks with you during those big childhood traumas that can sometimes extend into adolescence; a ball of fabric with a familiar smell that immediately cheers you up and makes you feel understood and loved. It almost makes you want to never grow up, just so you can hang on to that comfort!

And what about your first childhood pet? You've taught him to stay on the sidewalk and sit still so you can put his leash on, you've run through the woods together for hours on end, and he was always there barking happily when you got home from school. . . . All he's lacking is the gift of speech! He loves you without reservation. He taught you to share your steak at dinner and to accept certain inconveniences—the morning walk before you're really awake, and the evening walk when the rest of the family is lazing around in front of the TV. Children's books are full of stories of special friendships with animals. If you haven't read any of them, hurry up and start reading! Don't grow up without them! *Lassie, My Friend Flicka, Old Yeller*— these stories set an example. Some fictional misanthropes even prefer

spending time with animals to spending time with humans, but they're wrong to do so.

Friendship with an animal certainly is extraordinary: an animal will always listen and "nearly" understand everything. It can "nearly" tell us anything with a single look or a flick of the tongue. *Nearly*. This "nearly" makes all the difference because what we look for in a friend is someone who isn't scared to tell us what we don't always want to hear.

brothers and sisters:
beloved enemies

You've never been apart. Ever since she was born, or since you followed her into the world, you've shared everything—the same parents, the same memories, maybe even the same room. You've exchanged kisses and kicks, hugs and insults. But your closeness in age doesn't automatically mean you're friends. It can even discourage friendship because you share so much already. You spend so much time together that you don't want to see each other any more than you have to. You feel like you don't have anything more to learn about each other. But isn't taking the time to gradually discover new things about someone else one of the secrets of friendship?

A few years' difference can be a lot when you're a teen! The eldest is rocketing forward and doesn't have time to pay attention to the "little one" anymore; the youngest is running behind and rejects the sibling who has already turned his back on his recent childhood. Maybe you only stick together when you have to take a stand against your parents. The rest of the time, you're rivals; both of you still have to affirm your own identities. There's no doubt you love each other, but you'll deal with that later. Once siblings are older, they can often rediscover each other and become friends again.

much older siblings:

sometimes like friends, sometimes just like parents

It's a whole different story when there are more than a few years separating you from a sibling. When you were kids, you remained in your own worlds, with your own friends, activities, and school lives. You

ph4

didn't hang out together. But when you—the younger one—reach your teenage years, a relationship can begin to take shape. The older one—your brother or sister—can find satisfaction in playing the part of a parent: a closer, more approachable mentor, who can tell you what your real parents never would and can listen to what you would never tell your real parents. It's good for you to be listened to and supported by someone who, whether he or she likes it or not, has always been your "model" in the family. A new friendship can develop between the "big one" and the "little one." This can be a friendship that's safe from the rivalries and bickering that plague siblings in the same age range, and one that's reinforced by your shared family history. It can be a powerful friendship in which you both recognize you have things to tell and give each other.

your parents:
your friends?

Can mothers and fathers be friends to their children? Like true friends, they're always there, faithful to their duty. Like true friends, they can be attentive, thoughtful confidants. They know you well enough to read between the lines, even when you're making a face that would scare off a wild bear! Sometimes they even manage to give you advice without seeming to preach. But they're still your parents.

Even the coolest parents in the world sometimes have to set limits and put their feet down, even if they do it gently. It's not your best friend's job to tell you, "You really shouldn't have done that. This time you went too far"—it's your parents'. Although your friend can completely relate to your experience, she doesn't have any more perspective than you do. Like you, she has to test her limits to try life on for size. Your mother

and father have already gone through that and, because of this, they can help you to avoid the mistakes they made when they were young. They want to help you grow and think. Parents are supposed to teach you values. You can accept them, reject them, or tailor them to your needs. That's why teens often struggle with their families when these values start being questioned. What's important is to keep trying to communicate with your parents, even though you don't always agree with them. They're trying their best to guide you, but in the end you have to find the right path for yourself.

dear diary

"I hope I will be able to entrust you with all sorts of things, as I've never been able to do with anyone, and I hope you will be a great support to me."

With these words, Anne Frank began her diary on June 12, 1942. A few days later, on June 20, she continued: "I have a family, loving aunts, and a good home. No, on the surface I seem to have everything, except my one true friend. . . . This is why I've started the diary. To enhance the image of this long-awaited friend in my imagination, I don't want to jot down the facts in this diary the way most people would do, but I want the diary to be my friend, and I am going to call this friend *Kitty*."

Can a diary replace a real friend? According to Anne Frank, "Paper is more patient than people." It's true you never worry about boring your journal. You reveal yourself to it in ways you would never dare to do in any other circumstance. Line after line, you question yourself. Page after page, you search for that mysterious "me." Here and there, you find what you were looking for. In your diary, you can calm yourself or dig deeper into what's bothering you. But by dwelling on every intimate aspect of your life, you risk forgetting that growing up is about getting away from yourself and moving toward others.

A flesh-and-blood friend can respond to you and help you turn the page. As great a friend as a diary may be, building relationships with people will ultimately be more satisfying and rewarding. Enjoy writing in your diary every day, but don't forget how great it is to get a hug from a friend when you're feeling down.

mentors

Anybody who experiences friendship with a mentor will remain deeply affected by it. Like that high school kid who becomes friends with his uncle who has a master's degree in engineering, and decides that he, too, wants to be an engineer one day. Or that rebellious teen who becomes so close with her new English teacher that now she's following in her footsteps. Friendships between teenagers and young adults—someone halfway in age between you and your parents—are irreplaceable. They don't stop you from experiencing everything you need to shape your future personality. They don't deprive you of eagerly anticipated discoveries or severe disappointments. But they can fill you with positive energy and make you stronger. They catapult you forward. Never pitying or preachy, they're not like your parents, who, however available and attentive they may be, always seem to take the high road when they talk about their experiences and their parental responsibilities. If you ask an older friend for advice, he'll tell you what he thinks, even at the risk of making you unhappy or annoying you. Yet

you accept it, because it comes from someone you respect. These grown-up friends don't seem as out of touch as adults who have comfortably settled into their couches. They haven't abandoned their youth yet, but they're probably not consumed by acne attacks or growing pains, either. To your parents' great relief, these friends can guide you in a positive direction. Finally, their child is identifying with an adult!

arguments and complications

It was going to happen sooner or later . . . You were telling your friend about your weekend at Grammy's and Pop's and suddenly she interrupted you by saying, "You're just a hypocrite! You spend your time criticizing them, but you take advantage of their house in the country!" Then it was too late. You were overcome with anger and started spitting

out sentences, each one nastier than the last. "*You're* the hypocrite! You say you're my friend, but you always take the other side! What's the use of having a friend like you, you're always criticizing me!"

Poorly timed comments, misunderstood gestures, boy trouble or girl trouble, big ideological discussions—there are countless ways for friendships to get complicated! These misunderstandings are part of growing up and having relationships. Just remember to keep talking it out—that's what friends are for.

betrayal

You can't believe it. You put all your confidence in your friend. You used to tell him everything, until he acted like such a loser at that party. He started drinking to show off, and then he started hitting on the only girl in school you really liked, even though he knew you liked her. One thing's for sure: you'll never talk to him again. You're disgusted, betrayed, and disappointed. You invested your friendship in the wrong person. Don't worry, this guy will eventually fall off your radar and you'll find a friend who's worthy of you. Some friendships need to be spiced up with the occasional good-natured teasing. But does that mean we should accept anything in the name of friendship? No. Dependency and obedience are not the roots of friendship! And true friends don't manipulate you or make you forget your own values. For example, what's the point of smoking, just to be like her? Or of going out with a girl, to be like him? It's great to share the same experiences, but you don't always have to have the same outlook. Should you let a friend make racist comments when you know it's wrong? No way! That wouldn't help you, him, or your friendship.

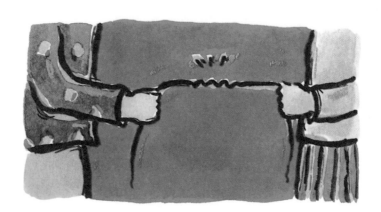

moving away?

What a disaster! Your dad just got a new job five hundred miles away. It's a promotion for him, but a demotion to depression for you. You're shipping out at the end of the year! You tried everything in your power to convince him to stay, but no dice. His career comes before your friendships. What about your best friend? He says you can write to her. "After all, five hundred miles isn't so far. She can come to visit, and we'll buy you a plane ticket to go see her." You'd think he never had a friend in his life, or that he's forgotten what it's like! But maybe he really doesn't have a choice about moving. Consider that, even though it won't make you feel better, or bring your best friend back. Adults frequently underestimate teenagers' pain.

They tell themselves that time heals all wounds. Sometimes, yes, but separation from a true friend can be incredibly difficult, like a bad breakup.

But distance does not need to put an end to your friendships. Phone calls, letters, little gifts, invitations—there are millions of ways to overcome it. After the first few months, you'll know if your friendship will survive. Either it will gradually disintegrate or, on the contrary, be reinforced by the distance. You and your friend may each rediscover its importance and intensity.

In either case, you still have the right to new friendships. Some people are scared of losing another friend, and prefer to shelter themselves. They'll have acquaintances, but no friends. They've decided not to have any ever again. Or worse, they feel incapable of making friends. They're too depressed. Other people, however, develop a gift for making new friends. Over the course of their many moves, they've learned to be open to others and have acquired an excellent ability to adapt. They know what you need to do to enter a group: make people laugh, be interested in everything, and don't get on anyone's bad side by making radical statements. They have enough experience to know that once you've figured out how to make one friend, you can do it again, as many times as you need to. The idea isn't necessarily to become a social butterfly, but simply to continue giving for the pleasure of receiving, and to know how to receive something in exchange for the pleasure of giving. Isn't that what friendship is all about?

past, present, and future:
friends forever?

They say that love passes while friendship remains. Is that true? Is it that simple? Do friendships "work" just because we want them to?

Have you ever had a friendship that came to an end? Maybe it reached a natural conclusion—like a friendship that lasts for just one summer while you're away together at camp—or maybe, after several disagreements, you gradually distanced yourself from someone you thought was a friend but really wasn't. Who says you can't *learn* how to be a friend? Aren't you allowed to make mistakes? When you learn how to solve new math problems in school, you don't ace them right away, because you need practice! And friendship is certainly more complicated than a math problem, especially when you're a teenager and, as you very well know, your personality is evolving nearly every day. Your body, head, and heart are growing and changing at varying speeds, and your friends are changing, too, but not necessarily at the same rate. So your connection, which might have been perfect a year ago, might suddenly be gone when you return from a vacation, or after an important event in your life. It's no more your fault than it is your friend's. Your paths have simply diverged. That doesn't mean that the friendship was meaningless. You were both enriched by it, and you learned a great deal from each other. When you're a teenager, a real friendship doesn't necessarily last a long time, nor is it exclusive. You can have several friends at once, all of whom are different people who you hang out with for different reasons.

Friendship is like a journey that teaches you about yourself. Step by step, you learn to be tolerant, to listen, to be available, and to trust. Just like a romantic relationship, it can take a long time to find the right friends. You don't always hit the jackpot the first time around, but once you do, you have to hold on to your winnings!

quotes

"A man who strives for happiness will also strive to share a friendship, an exchange which heightens man's awareness of his existence."
—CICERO (first century B.C.E.)

"In true friendship, all is clear and all is peaceful; friends have a common understanding of the words they speak."
—FRANÇOIS MAURIAC (*THE YOUNG MAN*)

"The only way to have a friend is to be one."
—EMERSON (*FRIENDSHIP*)

"To have friends is to be rich."
—RIMBAUD

"There is a friend that sticks closer than a brother."
—THE BIBLE

"Friendship doubles joy and cuts grief in half."
—BACON

suggestions for further reading

Auderset, Marie-José. *Walking Tall: How to Build Confidence and Be the Best You Can Be*. Amulet Books.

Carlson, Richard. *Don't Sweat the Small Stuff for Teens*. Hyperion.

Carnegie, Donna Dale. *How to Win Friends and Influence People for Teen Girls*. Fireside.

Clément, Claude and Melissa Daly. *Don't Be Shy: How to Fit in, Make Friends, and Have Fun—Even if You Weren't Born Outgoing*. Amulet Books.

Covey, Sean. *The 7 Habits of Highly Effective Teens*. Fireside.

Musgrave, Susan, ed. *You Be Me: Friendship in the Lives of Teen Girls*. Annick Press.

Perrier, Pascale. *Flying Solo: How to Soar Above Your Lonely Feelings, Make Friends, and Find the Happiest You*. Amulet Books.

Taylor, Julie. *The Girls' Guide to Friends: Straight Talk for Teens on Making Close Pals, Creating Lasting Ties, and Being an All-Around Great Friend*. Three Rivers Press.

index

Odile Amblard has been the deputy editor in chief of *Okapi* magazine since 1997. Specializing in education, youth, and adolescence, she is the author of numerous books.

Andrée Prigent was educated at the École Régionale des Beaux-Arts in Rennes and is a commercial and editorial illustrator.